MW00981406

© 2011 by Barbour Publishing, Inc.

ISBN 978-1-61626-173-3

Published by Barbour Publishing, Inc., P.O. Box 719, Uhrichsville, Ohio 44683, www.barbourbooks.com

Our mission is to publish and distribute inspirational products offering exceptional value and biblical encouragement to the masses.

Member of the
Evangelical Christian
Publishers Association

Printed in China.

Princess
Promises

BARBOUR

As a child of God, you
are a princess in His
kingdom.
Yes, that's right—
a princess!

"I will be your
Father,
and you will be
my. . .daughters,
says the LORD
Almighty."

2 CORINTHIANS 6:18

Believe in your heart
that God will do what
He says—because He
always will!

No matter how bad today may be, remember that you can start over again tomorrow.

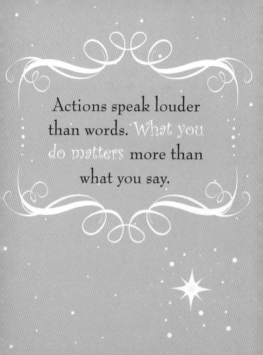

Actions speak louder than words. What you do matters more than what you say.

God created you—
He made you into the
unique, beautiful, and
talented individual
that you are.

The best plan for your life
is to live in Jesus.

Always look on the bright side. No matter what you're facing, there's always something to be thankful for.

Keep
praying.
God will
answer
when
the time
is right.

Work willingly at whatever you do, as though you were working for the Lord rather than for people.

COLOSSIANS 3:23

School might be boring.
Household chores stink.
But God asks you to do work
to bring glory to Him.

With God's help,
you can do anything!

True beauty
shines
from within.

Don't be afraid
to make mistakes.
Mistakes are part
of growing up.

Partner with God,
and you can
change the world.

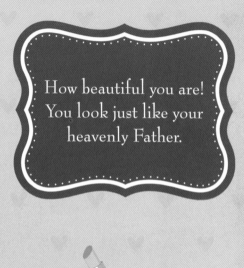

How beautiful you are!
You look just like your
heavenly Father.

Feeling lonely?
You don't have to!
God is with you every
moment of every day!

When we mess up,
God always gives us a
second chance.
All we have to do is ask.

There are bad things
all around, but God
will keep you strong.
Have confidence in Him!

*Two people are
better off
than one, for they
can help
each other succeed.*

Ecclesiastes 4:9

Your friends are priceless.
You are important to
them, and they to you.
Guard this treasure.

You don't have to do
anything special to earn
God's love.
He already loves you just
the way you are!

If you had a bank account in heaven, how much would you have saved? Jesus wants your treasures in heaven to account for more than your treasures on earth.

The best way to cheer
yourself up is to cheer
somebody else up.

MARK TWAIN

No matter how others
may treat you,

God always loves you.

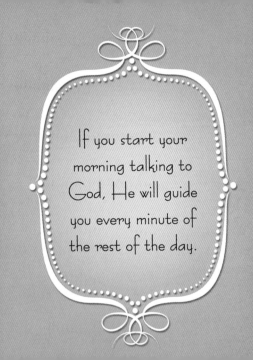

If you start your morning talking to God, He will guide you every minute of the rest of the day.

You don't have to grow
up on the inside.

All of you together are Christ's body, and each of you is a part of it.

1 Corinthians 12:27

When you're not sure
what to say, a hug is a good
place to start.

BONNIE JENSEN

Everyone has
a job to do.
God has given you
talents and special
interests that will
enable you to do what
He wants you to do.

God has given each of
you a gift from his great
variety of spiritual gifts.
Use them well to
serve one another.

1 PETER 4:10

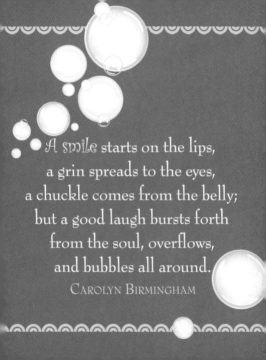

A smile starts on the lips,
a grin spreads to the eyes,
a chuckle comes from the belly;
but a good laugh bursts forth
from the soul, overflows,
and bubbles all around.

CAROLYN BIRMINGHAM

If you want
God, He is
there.
He is not
hiding. He
truly wants to
be with you.

God meets the needs of His
creation. So don't worry;
He's saved the very best for you.

*Don't you realize that
in a race everyone
runs, but only one
person gets the prize?
So run to win!*

1 CORINTHIANS 9:24

It is better to admit a
mistake than to hide it.

Everything around me
may change, but our
God is changeless!

You go before me and follow me.
You place your hand of blessing
on my head.

PSALM 139:5

Growing a plant is
a good way to show
you're responsible
enough for a pet.

Look forward to
tomorrow's opportunities.

Mix a little foolishness
with your serious plans.
It is lovely to be silly at
the right moment.

HORACE

There is
no such
thing as
too many
friends.

Let Jesus be
your best friend.

When someone
hurts your
feelings, forgive
him. It will
make God
happy.

When you're upset, let
God be your joy. Your
delight in Him will give
you the boost you need.

Charm is deceptive, and beauty does not last; but a woman who fears the LORD will be greatly praised.

PROVERBS 31:30

Worldly women may be *attractive* and *powerful* now, but true loveliness belongs to women who love God.

How do you treat
your family?
Your friends?
God says your love
should show others
His love every day.

Are you a daughter of the King? Then you have a home in heaven for all eternity!

God's love for
you is so big,
you can't
measure it.

Walking with a friend in
the dark is better than
walking alone in the *light*.

HELEN KELLER

When you feel
like singing,
share your song
loudly!

A real friend warms
you by her presence,
trusts you with
her secrets,
and remembers
you in her prayers.

UNKNOWN

God is like a shield that protects you. Tell Him today how much you love Him for keeping you safe.

Wear your
favorite outfit when
you're feeling down.

Cheerfulness brings
sunshine to the soul and
drives away the shadows
of anxiety.

Hannah Whitall Smith

It is pleasing to God whenever you rejoice or laugh from the bottom of your heart.

MARTIN LUTHER

Patience doesn't come easy,
but it's worth the effort.

*People with understanding
control their anger;
a hot temper shows great
foolishness.*

PROVERBS 14: 29

God's
agreement
with you is
as simple as
this: Trust in
Him, accept
the forgiveness
gift of Jesus,
and you're part
of His family.

Don't give up no matter
how hard things get.
Keep on keepin' on, princess!

God has amazing
plans for your life.

{ Being modest doesn't
mean being out of style. }

God answers every invitation
from His children—no matter
how small the gathering.

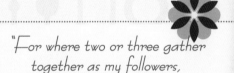

"For where two or three gather
together as my followers,
I am there among them."

MATTHEW 18:20

What's the best thing
about love? Love rooted
in Jesus lasts forever.

Don't be so hasty to
trade your sneakers
and play clothes for
high heels and lipstick.
Everything has its
moment and purpose.
You are right where
God wants you to be. . . .
Enjoy it!

Mark out a straight path for your feet; stay on the safe path.

PROVERBS 4:26

A little kindness. . .
goes a long, long way.

Respect for your parents is required by God. He put you together for a purpose. Obey Him, and He will bless you.

Are you
weak?
Fear not;
God is
strong.
He offers
His strength
to you.

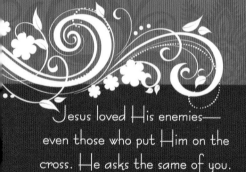

Jesus loved His enemies—
even those who put Him on the
cross. He asks the same of you.
Will you listen?

Smile and thank God for the fine job He did in making you His princess.

You might think that no one understands you. But God does. He made you, and He knows you *better than anyone else.*

"And the very hairs
on your head are all
numbered."

MATTHEW 10:30